MONSTERS

GODZILLA

BY ADAM WOOG

KIDHAVEN
PRESS™

THOMSON
————★————™
GALE

San Diego • Detroit • New York • San Francisco • Cleveland
New Haven, Conn. • Waterville, Maine • London • Munich

Acknowledgements:
Special thanks to J.D. Lees of G-Fan magazine and
James Bailey for research help.

Dedication:
For Clyde Horn, longtime Godzilla fan.

For more information, contact
The Gale Group, Inc.
27500 Drake Rd.
Farmington Hills, MI 48331-3535
Or you can visit our Internet site at http://www.gale.com

LIBRARY OF CONGRESS CATALOGING-IN-PUBLICATION DATA

Woog, Adam, 1953–
  Godzilla / by Adam Woog.
    p. cm. — (Monsters series)
  Includes bibliographical references and index.
    ISBN 0-7377-2616-4
    1. Godzilla films—History and criticism—Juvenile literature. I. Title. II. Monsters series (KidHaven Press)
    QPN1995.9.G63W66 2004
    791.43'67—dc22
 	
                                                                2004003743

Printed in the United States of America

CONTENTS

CHAPTER 1
King of the Japanese
Movie Monsters   4

CHAPTER 2
Godzilla Comes to Life   13

CHAPTER 3
The Many Moods of Godzilla   22

CHAPTER 4
Godzilla Lives!   32

Notes   40
Glossary   42
For Further Exploration   43
Index   45
Picture Credits   47
About the Author   48

CHAPTER 1

King of the Japanese Movie Monsters

In Japan, movies about giant monsters have been popular for many years. Rodan, a huge creature with wings and sharp teeth, and Mothra, a giant moth, are just two examples of the many strange and exciting monsters that roam through *kaiju eiga*. (*Kaiju eiga* is Japanese for "monster movie.")

But of all the Japanese movie monsters, Godzilla is the king. He was one of the first of the Japanese movie monsters, and he is still the strongest of them all. He has survived dozens of battles, some against several monsters at the same time. Also, Godzilla excites the imagination of his audiences—but not just because of his destructive power. In some movies Godzilla seems almost human in his concern for the environment and smaller, more helpless monsters. According to Godzilla expert J.D. Lees, "Radioactive terror, force of nature, thirty-story defender of Earth. . . . Godzilla is all these to be sure. But it may be the glimpses we catch of Godzilla's human-like emotions that make him such an enduring and popular character around the world."[1]

Godzilla's first movie, *Godzilla, King of the Monsters*, appeared in 1954. In the fifty years since then, the big

Godzilla has been destroying towns and battling other monsters since his first movie appearance in 1954.

monster has starred in about two dozen more movies. They have all been wildly popular in Japan. Godzilla's fame and popularity have also spread around the world. Today he is a world-famous celebrity.

A Really Big Atomic Dinosaur

Godzilla is an invented dinosaur from prehistoric times. Over the years Godzilla's appearance has changed a little, but his basic looks have stayed the same. The monster is a combination of two dinosaurs. He looks mostly like a *Tyrannosaurus rex,* but he also has plates on his back like those of a *Stegosaurus.*

Godzilla is enormously tall. He stands higher than many buildings, and over time he has grown even bigger. In his first movie, Godzilla was about 160 feet

Godzilla battles Mothra, a giant moth. Whenever he fights other monsters he always wins.

(50 meters) high. In more recent movies, he is about 300 feet (100 meters) high.

Godzilla is also very strong. He can easily crush buildings or cars by stomping his feet or swishing his tail. He picks up trains as if they were toys. In addition, Godzilla can breathe out a deadly atomic ray. He uses this ray to attack his enemies.

Many people think Godzilla is green because Godzilla toys and models are often green. However, the monster is charcoal gray in all of the Japanese movies.

GODZILLA IS BORN!

Godzilla was invented because a Japanese movie executive, Tomoyuki Tanaka, was desperate for a hit in a hurry. Tanaka was a producer at Toho Studios, one of Japan's biggest movie studios. In 1954 he tried to make a war movie in Indonesia. However, the Indonesian government did not give him permission. The project had to be cancelled.

The war movie was supposed to be that year's big project for Toho. Tanaka needed another project quickly. On the plane back to Tokyo, he thought about what to do. Looking down at the ocean, the producer began imagining a story about a monster living under the sea.

During the 1950s, monster movies were big hits. Among the most popular were films about werewolves, vampires, and the giant ape King Kong. Tanaka knew a monster movie could be a success.

An Atomic Monster

Tanaka had an idea to make his movie better than the many other monster films. Horror movies about the terrible effects of atomic radiation were also very popular during the 1950s. For example, in the American movie *The Beast from 20,000 Fathoms* a giant creature, released from Arctic ice by a nuclear test, destroys New York. Tanaka thought he could connect a monster story to people's fears about atomic energy.

At the time Japan was very sensitive to this subject. Fewer than ten years earlier, in 1945, American planes had dropped the first atomic bombs on the Japanese cities of Nagasaki and Hiroshima. The bombs helped to speed up the end of World War II, but peace came at a terrible price. The blasts killed an estimated two hundred thousand Japanese citizens and injured or sickened many more.

These horrors were fresh in the minds of Japanese citizens in 1954. Tanaka guessed that audiences would react strongly to a movie about a destructive monster created by radiation. He recalled, "The thesis [idea] was very simple. What if a dinosaur sleeping in the Southern Hemisphere had been awakened and transformed into a giant by the bomb? What if it attacked Tokyo?"[2]

Combining a Gorilla and a Whale

Tanaka and his coworkers discussed several possible forms their monster could take. For a while they

An atomic bomb blast wakes up Godzilla from a long sleep at the bottom of the SouthPacific Ocean.

thought it might be a giant octopus. They finally settled on a dinosaur-like creature.

In the story they created, the dinosaur has been **dormant** (not active) in the South Pacific Ocean for millions of years. Then atomic bomb testing wakes

In his first movie, Godzilla comes out of the ocean and nearly destroys Tokyo, Japan.

him up. These atomic blasts also change the creature and give him awesome radioactive powers.

The monster destroys a fishing boat and heads to Japan to destroy Tokyo. After a huge battle the monster is driven back into the ocean by military jets. Then a scientist uses a powerful weapon, the Oxygen Destroyer, to kill the creature. The scientist chooses to die as well. He hopes that the secret of his Oxygen Destroyer will die with him, so that no one will ever use this terrible weapon again.

As they created their story, the moviemakers chose a name for their monster. In Japanese, *Godzilla* is pro-

nounced *Go-ji-ra*. According to some sources, this was the nickname of a big, heavyset Toho employee.

In any case, it is an invented word combining the names of two animals: the English word *gorilla* and the Japanese word for whale, *kujira*. The filmmakers thought the name suited their new creature well. Eiji Tsuburaya, a special-effects expert, recalls, "We just adopted it for our monster. It caught on and certainly has immortalized him!"[3]

"RUN FOR COVER"

Later Godzilla movies changed his history a little, but they are all similar in some ways. Each begins with the creature being quiet. In the first movie, he is sleeping deep in the South Pacific. In some later films, he is living with other creatures in a faraway place called Monster Island. In still other films, he has been trapped inside a volcano or another resting place.

In every film Godzilla escapes. No matter where he is when that happens, he always makes his way to Japan. Usually, he goes on a **rampage**. In the first movie he terrified Tokyo, Japan's biggest city. In later movies he destroyed other large cities, such as Osaka and Nagoya. A familiar sound in a Godzilla movie is authorities using loudspeakers to warn people that the monster is loose once again: "Run for cover. Run for cover. Godzilla is now in the suburbs. He is moving this way. Run for cover."[4]

Sometimes Godzilla's power is used for evil, sometimes for good. In either case, it is always used.

In this movie poster, Godzilla uses his radioactive powers to destroy a Japanese city.

A Godzilla movie would not be a Godzilla movie without several huge battles. Sometimes Godzilla destroys everything in sight. Sometimes he fights against other monsters that are threatening the world. And sometimes he battles evil versions of himself.

Godzilla

CHAPTER 2

Godzilla Comes to Life

To many audiences today, the early Godzilla movies seem rough, crude, and unpolished. There are several reasons for this. For one thing, in the 1950s budgets for films in Japan were much smaller than in America. Compared to Hollywood films, the early Godzilla movies cost very little.

Also, Godzilla's makers were unable to use the advanced equipment and techniques moviemakers today can use. Today's movies are full of eye-popping special effects. These are created using techniques such as powerful, computer-generated graphic effects.

By contrast, the special effects in Godzilla films were made simply. Computer graphics were still many

Modern Godzilla movies use computer-generated special effects to make Godzilla look very scary.

years in the future when Godzilla was born. His creators had to find other ways to create their illusions.

BUILDING GODZILLA

To bring the story to life, the filmmakers had to decide exactly what their monster should look like. Eiji Tsuburaya, who was in charge of special effects, started by building about ten small clay models. Each model gave the filmmakers an idea of what Godzilla could look like. They chose a design that combined elements of real dinosaurs, such as the spiked back of a *Stegosaurus* and the general shape of a *Tyrannosaurus rex*.

Using the model, the special-effects team built a human-size Godzilla suit. Unlike today's movies, for

Godzilla

which computers can create a lifelike monster, an actor in a Godzilla suit played the creature. This technique is called *suitmation*.

The suit was made of rubber and painted gray. To give it strength and bulk, Tsuburaya and his crew stuffed bamboo and foam between the outside layer and cloth lining. They also put a zipper in the back, so an actor could climb in and out.

"THE COSTUME CONTROLLED ME"

The actor's head came up as far as the monster's neck. Tiny holes were drilled there so that he could see and breathe. Godzilla's head was worn on the actor's head like a hat. From top

Godzilla's creators combined a Stegosaurus *(left) and a* Tyrannosaurus rex *(below) to make their monster.*

The early Godzilla was actually played by an actor wearing a two-hundred-pound rubber suit.

to bottom the suit was a little more than six feet high (two meters).

Moving the monster required the efforts of several people. The monster's mouth and eyes were moved by remote control. Technicians moved its tail with wires. The actor playing Godzilla moved the creature's arms and body. Haruo Nakajima, who played the monster in the first movie, recalled, "I studied the movements of large animals to re-create the lumbering walk of a large creature."[5]

The actor could only move slowly because the suit was very heavy. The first costume weighed about two hundred pounds (ninety kilograms), though later versions were a little lighter. The actor inside could

walk only about thirty feet (nine meters) before needing a rest. It was also extremely hot, especially under the bright lights needed for filming. Actors who played Godzilla usually lost at least twenty pounds (nine kilograms) during the several weeks it took to shoot a movie.

The suit was so uncomfortable that it could only be worn for a few minutes at a time. Ken Satsuma, who played Godzilla in many movies, was an outstanding athlete and in excellent physical shape. Nonetheless, he found the job challenging. Over the years he suffered a variety of misfortunes.

Satsuma often found it so difficult to breathe that he became dizzy. He suffered concussions several times by accidentally running into props on the set. On several occasions he nearly drowned while filming in pools of water meant to imitate the ocean. Satsuma also once suffered painful electrocution, when faulty wiring inside the suit shocked him. "I had a tough time. I felt that the costume controlled me,"[6] the actor remarked.

Miniatures and Sound Effects

In addition to making Godzilla himself, the filmmakers needed to create miniature sets for him to destroy. When filmed with the Godzilla actor looming over them, the tiny sets seemed real.

Tsuburaya and his crew built a number of these sets. Many were in $\frac{1}{24}$th scale. A model of a ten-story building would only be about four feet high

(1.2 meters). The sets included many tiny buildings and streets, complete with cars, tanks, and other objects. Together they formed a small version of Tokyo.

The models of things destined to be crushed by Godzilla were not just empty shells. If they were, they would not have looked realistic when stomped on. For example, the model creators built interiors into each floor of the buildings Godzilla destroyed. Also, miniature cars and trucks were made of cast iron, so they would seem more realistic when destroyed.

All of these miniatures had to be created in a very short time. Yoshio Irie, an assistant art director, recalls, "I don't think Toho's executives realized how time-consuming a process building all of the miniatures would be. We were given only three months to complete our work."[7] Considering the large amount of work involved, this was an extremely tight deadline.

Meanwhile, two important sound effects were created. They were devised by Akira Ifukube, who also composed the movie's sound track. He invented Godzilla's famous screeching roar by coating a leather glove with sticky resin, rubbing it over the strings of a double bass, and adding an echo. Ifukube also created the sound of Godzilla's heavy footsteps. He did this by beating a thick, knotted rope on a kettle drum.

A HIT

When it was finished, the film was called *Godzilla*. Because of the many special effects required, it was,

at the time, the most expensive movie ever made in Japan. The film was eagerly anticipated. When it came out people waited for hours to buy tickets.

Godzilla became one of the most popular films in Japan for 1954. In 1956 the movie (retitled *Godzilla, King of the Monsters*) was released in America. It was a hit there, too.

When the original Godzilla movie was released in the United States, it was changed for American audiences.

However, the movie was changed for American audiences. (This was true for later Godzilla movies as well.) The order of the scenes was different. Some scenes were dropped completely, and new scenes with American actors were added. Also, the movie was dubbed into English. That is, the voices of American actors were used instead of the originals. One of these American actors was a teenager named George Takei, who later played Sulu on *Star Trek*.

Moviegoers in America and Japan alike loved Godzilla. One fan was Steven Spielberg, who first saw the film when he was a boy. As millions of movie lovers know, Spielberg later honored Godzilla with the dinosaur monsters in his *Jurassic Park* series. Spielberg recalls, "*Godzilla* . . . was the most masterful of all the dinosaur movies because it made you believe it was really happening."[8]

SEQUELS

The first Godzilla movie was not meant to have a sequel. It was supposed to be a single movie, designed to make a strong statement about the dangers of atomic energy. Director Ishiro Honda recalls, "Believe it or not, we had no plans for a sequel and . . . hoped that the end of *Godzilla* was going to coincide with the end of nuclear testing."[9]

However, *Godzilla, King of the Monsters* was such a success that a sequel was immediately planned. In America this sequel was called *Godzilla Raids Again*. In it the creature returns to destroy Osaka,

Steven Spielberg, a fan of Godzilla, created his own dinosaur monsters for his Jurassic Park *movies.*

Japan's second-largest city, while battling another monster.

Many more movies followed. Toho Studios tried to kill the Godzilla character a few times, but his popularity was too great. He was always brought back to life for another adventure. Along the way, Godzilla underwent many changes.

CHAPTER 3

The Many Moods of Godzilla

In Godzilla's first movies he had little personality. His only purpose was to terrify and destroy. Survival was all that mattered to him.

Over the years, however, Godzilla changed. The monster's creators wanted to attract younger audiences and more female viewers. To make Godzilla more appealing to women and children, they added humor. They also made Godzilla less scary.

In some movies he became a hero by defending people against evil monsters. In other movies he acted like a parent, protecting younger monsters and teaching them how to act. Or he became an environmental warrior. In this role he protected nature from disaster.

Godzilla's looks changed too, reflecting changes in his personality. For example, in *Godzilla vs. Megalon,* he is supposed to be friendlier. His eyes are bigger and his cheeks are puffier. This Godzilla looks a little like a gentle, cute puppy.

GODZILLA THE DESTROYER

In the first movie, Godzilla is a purely destructive force created by foolish humans. The film warns that if humankind is not careful, it runs the risk of creating another Godzilla. In the movie a scientist remarks, "I cannot believe Godzilla was the last survivor of its species. If we continue nuclear testing, others of Godzilla's kind will appear again somewhere in the world."[10]

In the films that followed, this view of Godzilla changes a little. He is still terribly destructive. But

Godzilla's looks became less scary over the years to make him more appealing to women and children.

INCREDIBLE, UNSTOPPABLE TITAN OF TERROR
GODZILLA
It's Alive!
KING OF THE MONSTERS
CIVILIZATION CRUMBLES as its death rays blast a city of 6 million from the face of the earth!

people in these movies realize he is not simply an evil thing or simply a creation of humans. He is a force of nature, like a hurricane or an earthquake.

Seen in this way, a force such as Godzilla can never be defeated. It must simply be survived. As one character states, "Nature has a way sometimes of reminding . . . us of how puny we really are in the face of a tornado, an earthquake, or a Godzilla."[11]

GODZILLA THE HERO

Godzilla changed from being terrifying to being a friendly savior of humans with his fifth movie, *Ghidorah, the Three Headed Monster.* In this film and several that came after it, Godzilla is still a destructive force of nature. However, he is also a hero who saves humans from evil creatures. Sometimes these villains are other monsters from earth. Often, however, Godzilla's enemies are aliens or space monsters.

In *Godzilla vs. Gigan,* aliens try to take over the world. They summon two space monsters to destroy Tokyo. The aliens also lure Godzilla from his resting place, so they can kill him. But Godzilla battles the monsters and sends them back into space. Then he destroys the aliens before returning home.

While saving humanity Godzilla finds a special role as a hero to children. In *All Monsters Attack* Godzilla is seen only in a lonely boy's imagination.

Opposite: A destructive Godzilla levels a city in this 1956 movie poster.

In Ghidorah, the Three Headed Monster, *Godzilla battles evil monsters from earth and outer space in order to save humanity.*

The boy pretends he goes to remote Monster Island, where Godzilla lives with other monsters.

A strong and kindly Godzilla plays with the boy. Then, using the lessons he learned during this imaginary play, the boy (in real life) helps police catch some bank robbers. He also takes revenge on some bullies at school, proving he can defend himself without help.

GODZILLA THE PARENT

In several movies Godzilla becomes a parent. He proves to be a very good father. This is another ex-

ample of how Godzilla's creators wanted to make him appealing to children.

In *Son of Godzilla* weather-control experiments are taking place on a remote island. The experiments go wrong and cause monsters living on the island to grow to an enormous size. Meanwhile, an egg hatches and a cute baby Godzilla, called Minilla, is born. Minilla is Godzilla's son.

Godzilla arrives to take care of the baby. The two have many scenes together that make them seem almost human. For instance, Godzilla protects his son from the big, evil creatures. He also teaches Minilla

Godzilla has starred in more than two dozen very successful movies in the last fifty years.

how to breathe fire. (At first the baby can only blow smoke rings.)

Godzilla's role as a parent has been repeated several times. For example, in *Godzilla vs. Mechagodzilla II*, a young monster called Baby Godzilla appears. (This is a different character than Minilla.) He is the object of a huge battle between Godzilla and two other monsters, Mechagodzilla and Fire Rodan. Godzilla successfully fights to protect the younger monster.

Baby Godzilla reappears in *Godzilla vs. Space-Godzilla* and *Godzilla vs. Destroyer*. (In these films he is sometimes called Little Godzilla or Godzilla Junior.) As in the other movies, Godzilla must free his son from evil monsters. He also teaches Baby Godzilla how to act like an adult monster.

Godzilla's personality has changed many times since his first movie. Here, an evil Godzilla battles Orga in Godzilla 2000.

Godzilla the Eco-Warrior

Godzilla's personality changed in another way in the early 1970s. This had to do with ecology. Like many other countries, Japan was then experiencing serious environmental problems. Pollution was wrecking the countryside and hurting people. Saving the planet became a major concern.

In response to this, the moviemakers at Toho made Godzilla into a protector of the earth's environment. This can clearly be seen in *Godzilla vs. Hedorah* (also known as *Godzilla vs. the Smog Monster*). Terrible creatures made of a living mineral appear. They feed on industrial waste, grow larger, and come together to form a single, giant monster called Hedorah.

Hedorah can spit poison that rusts buildings and turns people into skeletons. It attacks a group of young people who are attending an environmental festival near Fuji, the highest mountain in Japan and a symbol of the nation's natural beauty. Godzilla comes to the rescue. Working with the Japanese military, he succeeds in destroying Hedorah. Godzilla then returns to his home on Monster Island.

Back to Being Bad

Not everyone liked the changes in Godzilla's personality. Many of the monster's fans hated them. They did not like him being cute or comical. They wanted Godzilla to be scary again!

The Many Moods of Godzilla   29

In the end the executives at Toho decided that trying to make Godzilla into a likable hero was not working. Starting in 1985 with *The Return of Godzilla* (also called *Godzilla 1985*), Godzilla stopped being friendly. Once again he became a terrifying and destructive force.

This trend has continued with such recent films as *Godzilla, Mothra and King Ghidorah: Giant Monsters All-Out Attack.* In this movie Godzilla is clearly evil, and two other monsters must save Japan from him. Here, Godzilla does not just kill people accidentally. He does it on purpose. For example, in one scene Godzilla stops his rampage so that he can direct his deadly, radioactive breath toward helpless people.

Throughout his many changes in personality, from bad to good to bad again, Godzilla has remained popular. His fame extends far beyond just those who love Japanese monster movies. Godzilla has become familiar around the world as a genuine celebrity.

CHAPTER 4

Godzilla Lives!

Today Godzilla still rules in the world of Japanese monster movies. In Japan millions of loyal fans continue to flock to theaters to see his latest adventures. Since 1989 each new Godzilla film has been among the top five money earners for Toho Studios for that year.

Godzilla also continues to have millions of fans in other countries. By 1984, the monster's thirtieth anniversary, an estimated 65 million people worldwide had seen a Godzilla movie. And hundreds of thousands had joined one of the many Godzilla fan clubs.

There are no signs that the big monster will slow down. Koichi Kawakita, a special-effects expert who has worked on many Godzilla films, recently remarked, "We . . . produce each new Godzilla movie with the expectation that the series will continue on for another forty years."[12]

Meanwhile, Godzilla's fame has moved far beyond the movie theater. Even people who are not interested in monster films know who he is. He has become a familiar figure nearly everywhere in the world.

New Godzilla Sightings in America

Home video is an important way in which Godzilla's life has spread beyond the theater. This is especially

Godzilla continues to appear in movies more than fifty years after his first movie.

Although not all of Godzilla's movies have been released in American theaters, all are available on video and DVD.

true in the United States, since not all of Godzilla's movies have been shown in American theaters. All of the Godzilla movies are available on VHS or DVD.

There have been many other Godzilla sightings in America in the decades since he made his first appearance. In the 1970s the creature starred in a series of Saturday morning cartoons. These showed the cute side of Godzilla. For example, his sidekick was a sweet baby monster called Godzooky.

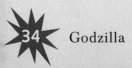

More Godzilla Sightings in America

In 1992 Godzilla was also featured in a famous advertising campaign in America. Nike produced a series of ads in which basketball legend Charles Barkley and Godzilla battled each other, one-on-one, across downtown Tokyo. The two later fought it out in a special comic book as well.

In 1998 the monster made still another American appearance. That year, the only Godzilla movie ever produced outside of Japan was released. The new movie, which starred Matthew Broderick, was simply called *Godzilla*.

It had some spectacular special effects, and it was a hit with many people. However, critics generally

Spectacular special effects made 1998's Godzilla *a hit with many moviegoers.*

disliked it, and most serious Godzilla fans passionately hated it. In their opinion it was not true to the spirit of the original monster. They ridiculed the film by calling it "GINO"–Godzilla in Name Only.

A Deep Sea of Collectibles

In addition to seeing movies, fans can collect Godzilla **memorabilia**, or collectible items. Buying, selling, and collecting Godzilla memorabilia has become a passionate hobby for thousands of fans around the world. In fact, according to some sources, Toho Studios earns more money from **licensing** Godzilla's image on these collectible items than it does from the movies themselves. (Licensing means letting people use an image for a fee.)

Anyone who wants to collect Godzilla-related material can choose from a wide assortment. Collectors buy, sell, or trade such items as Godzilla dolls, action figures, posters, puzzles, video games, purses, bed sheets, books, magazines, comic books, lunch boxes, T-shirts, and remote-control toys. There are even Godzilla toilet-paper holders and Godzilla cigarette lighters. Press the cigarette lighter's fins and a flame shoots out from its mouth.

Trading cards are especially popular examples of Godzilla collectibles. Over the years Toho has produced many sets of these cards. They show colorful scenes, such as original poster art and famous moments from Godzilla's films. Some cards have 3-D images and other special graphics.

Honoring Godzilla

In addition to videos and collectible items, Godzilla is kept alive in several other ways. For instance, there are many Internet Web sites devoted to him. These are mostly maintained by fans. Toho Studios maintains its own site about Godzilla and other monsters,

Thousands of Godzilla fans around the world collect memorabilia such as this tin toy.

written in Japanese. There are also several magazines about Japanese movie monsters. One is *G-Fan,* which is edited by a Canadian Godzilla expert, J.D. Lees.

Godzilla fans around the world keep in touch in several ways. One way is through the Internet. Also, they can meet at various Godzilla fan conventions. Really serious fans can even join special Godzilla tours of Japan. These groups visit many of the top sites associated with the monster's battles, such as Tokyo Tower, the Lake Kawaguchi area, and Osaka Castle. Because it is a busy, working movie studio, Toho does not give tours.

Godzilla has received a number of honors over the years. A statue in Tokyo's Hibiya Park honors his contributions to Japan's film industry. Los Angeles has

A statue in Hibiya Park in Tokyo honors Godzilla's place in Japanese film.

twice declared a Godzilla Week: in 1996, to honor Godzilla's fortieth anniversary in America, and in 2000 to celebrate the release of *Godzilla 2000*. In 1996, MTV presented the big monster with a Lifetime Achievement Award for his contributions to popular culture.

Godzilla has even entered religious life in America. In the small town of Zillah, Washington, the local Church of God officially declared itself the Church of God, Zillah. In a light-hearted mood, church members built a huge statue of Godzilla in front of their place of worship. They also sell T-shirts celebrating their special church name.

A Survivor

Godzilla was never supposed to last beyond one movie. He was never meant to become a hero or a celebrity. In fact, Godzilla was supposed to die on several occasions. He has always come back to life, however, because his great popularity demands it. Godzilla expert David Kalat comments, "Godzilla has withstood every attack alone and friendless, yet he survives."[13]

And so, instead of being forgotten or killed off, Godzilla lives. He remains one of the world's most famous creatures. To his millions of fans, Godzilla will always be the king of the monsters.

Notes

Chapter 1: King of the Japanese Movie Monsters

1. J.D. Lees, e-mail interview with author.
2. Quoted in David Kalat, *A Critical History and Filmography of Toho's Godzilla Series.* Jefferson, NC: McFarland, 1997, p. 13.
3. Quoted in "Alternative Sci.lang.japan," www. csse.monash.edu.au.
4. Quoted in Leonard Wolf, *Monsters: Twenty Terrible and Wonderful Beasts from the Classic Dragon and Colossal Minotaur to King Kong and the Great Godzilla.* San Francisco: Straight Arrow Books, 1974, p. 81.

Chapter 2: Godzilla Comes to Life

5. Quoted in "KAIJU CONVERSATIONS: An Interview with Godzilla: Haruo Nakajima," www.dalekempire.com.
6. Quoted in J.D. Lees and Marc Cerasini, *The Official Godzilla Compendium.* New York: Random House, 1998, p. 57.
7. Quoted in "Monster Zero News," www.clubtokyo. org.
8. Quoted in Kalat, *A Critical History,* p. 50.
9. Quoted in Kalat, *A Critical History,* p. 36.

Chapter 3: The Many Moods of Godzilla

10. Quoted in Kalat, *A Critical History*, p. 19.
11. Quoted in "Barry's Temple of Godzilla," www.stomptokyo.com.

Chapter 4: Godzilla Lives!

12. Quoted in "Monster Zero News."
13. Kalat, *A Critical History*, p. 244.

GLOSSARY

dormant: Asleep or inactive.

kaiju eiga: Means "monster movie" in Japanese. Pronounced *kai-joo ae-ga.*

licensing: Letting people use a copyrighted image for a fee. A copyright law protects something to keep people from using it without permission.

memorabilia: Items related to a specific subject.

rampage: Violent, destructive behavior.

FOR FURTHER EXPLORATION

BOOKS

Kazuhisa Iwata, *Godzilla*. Milwaukie, OR: Dark Horse Comics, 1995. A book in comic-book form, based on the movie *Godzilla 1985*.

J.D. Lees and Marc Cerasini, *The Official Godzilla Compendium*. New York: Random House, 1998. A nicely illustrated collection all about the big monster, by two Godzilla experts.

James Preller, *Godzilla*. New York: Scholastic, 1998. A storybook based on the 1998 American movie version of *Godzilla*.

WEB SITES

Barry's Temple of Godzilla (www.stomptokyo. com). A site maintained by a fan, with lots of information on all the Godzilla movies.

Kaijufan Online (www.kaijufan.com). This is a site maintained by a New York City fan, helped out by contributors around the world, about Japanese monster movies in general. The text is not written for young readers, but many sections are well illustrated.

Origami Monsters (www.occn.zaq.ne.jp). This site has clear instructions on making Godzilla and other monsters using origami, the art of Japanese paper folding.

Rodan's Roost (http://rodansroost.com). A huge site maintained by fans of Japanese movie monsters, including Godzilla. Includes games, such as a Godzilla jigsaw puzzle, and an excellent section of classic posters.

INDEX

actors, 16–17, 20
advertisements, 35
All Monsters Attack, 25–26
appearance, 6–7, 14, 23
atomic bombs, 8, 9–10
awards, 36–39

Baby Godzilla, 28
Barkley, Charles, 35
Beast from 20,000 Fathoms, The, 8
Broderick, Matthew, 35

cartoons, 34
Church of God, 39
color, 7
computer graphics, 13–14

DVDs, 34

fan conventions, 38
Fire Rodan, 28

G-Fan (magazine), 38
Ghidorah, the Three Headed Monster, 25
Godzilla, 31, 35–36
Godzilla, King of the Monsters, 5, 7–10, 18–20
Godzilla, Mothra and King Ghidorah: Giant Monsters All-

Out Attack, 31
Godzilla movies
changes in, 22–23
common parts to, 11, 12
first, 5
idea for, 7–9
number of, 6
special effects in, 14–18
see also specific movies
Godzilla 1985, 31
Godzilla 2000, 39
Godzilla Raids Again, 20–21
Godzilla vs. Destroyer, 28
Godzilla vs. Gigan, 25–26
Godzilla vs. Hedorah, 29
Godzilla vs. Mechagodzilla II, 28
Godzilla vs. Megalon, 23
Godzilla vs. Space-Godzilla, 28
Godzilla vs. the Smog Monster, 29
Godzilla Weeks, 39
Godzooky, 34

Hedorah, 29
height, 6–7
Hibiya Park, (Tokyo, Japan), 38–39
home videos, 33–34
Honda, Ishiro, 20
honors, 38–39
horror movies, 8

Internet, 37–38
Irie, Yoshio, 18

Kalat, David, 39
Kawakita, Koichi, 32–33

Lees, J.D., 5, 38

Mechagodzilla, 28
memorabilia, 36
miniatures, 17–18
Minilla, 27–28
monster movies, 4, 7
Mothra, 4
MTV Lifetime Achievement
 Award, 39

Nakajima, Haruo, 16
name, 10–11
Nike, 35

Oxygen Destroyer, 10

personality, 4–5
 as destroyer, 23, 25, 31
 as eco-warrior, 29
 as hero, 25–26
 as parent, 26–28
popularity, 6, 19, 32–33,
 36–39

Return of Godzilla, The, 31
Rodan, 4

Satsuma, Ken, 17
sequels, 20–21
Son of Godzilla, 27–28
sound effects, 18
special effects
 American Godzilla,
  35–36
 current, 13–14
 miniatures, 17–18
 suitmation, 15–17
Spielberg, Steven, 20
strength, 7, 11–12
suitmation, 15–17

Takei, George, 20
Tanaka, Tomoyuki, 7
Toho Studios, 7, 21
trading cards, 36
Tsuburaya, Eiji, 11, 14

United States, 19–20,
 35–36

VHS, 34
videos, 33–34

Zillah, Washington, 39

Picture Credits

Cover: © Photofest
Courtesy of Aylon.org, 9 (inset), 24
© Bettmann/CORBIS, 5
© B.S.P.I./CORBIS, 38
© Ely Kish/Canadian Museum of Nature, 15
   (bottom)
© Mark McCreery, 15 (inset)
© Louis K. Meisel Gallery/CORBIS, 37
Courtesy of Monstercon 2004, 34 (both)
© CLOSE MURRAY/CORBIS SYGMA, 21
© Photofest, 6, 10, 12, 14, 16, 19, 23, 26, 27, 28,
   30, 33, 35
© Royalty Free/CORBIS, 9

ABOUT THE AUTHOR

Adam Woog has written more than forty books for adults, young adults, and children. He lives in Seattle, Washington, with his wife and their daughter. He and his wife had a six-foot inflatable Godzilla at their wedding reception.